250 Fascinating Facts about LDS Temples

Rebekah Pitts

CFI • An Imprint of Cedar Fort, Inc. • Springville, Utah

ISBN 13: 978-1-4621-2297-4

Published by CFI, an imprint of Cedar Fort, Inc.
2373 W. 700 S., Springville, UT 84663
Distributed by Cedar Fort, Inc. www.cedarfort.com

LIBRARY OF CONGRESS CATALOGING-IN-PUBLICATION DATA

Names: Pitts, Rebekah, 1977- author.
Title: 250 fascinating facts about LDS temples / Rebekah Pitts.
Other titles: Two hundred fifty fascinating facts about LDS temples
Description: Springville, Utah : CFI, an imprint of Cedar Fort, Inc., [2018]
Identifiers: LCCN 2018027616 (print) | LCCN 2018015871 (ebook) | ISBN 9781462122974 (perfect bound : alk. paper) | ISBN 9781462129942 (epub, pdf, mobi)
Subjects: LCSH: Mormon temples--Miscellanea.
Classification: LCC BX8643.T4 P58 2018 (ebook) | LCC BX8643.T4 (print) | DDC 246/.9589332--dc23
LC record available at https://lccn.loc.gov/2018027616

Cover and interior layout design by Markie Riley
Cover design © 2018 Cedar Fort, Inc.
Edited by Kaitlin Barwick

Printed in the United States of America

10 9 8 7 6 5 4 3 2 1

Printed on Acid-free paper

In ancient times,
TEMPLES
dotted the earth.

The word TEMPLE appears 191 times in the Bible.

The Latin word for temple,

templum,

literally translates as

"the house of the Lord."

There is a temple in heaven.

THE FIRST TEMPLES WERE NOT BUILDINGS MADE OF WOOD, FABRIC, OR STONE.

THEY WERE OUTSIDE, IN THE WILDERNESS, AND ON THE MOUNTAINTOPS.

AFRICAN SAINTS SAVED UP TO 6 MONTHS' WORTH OF INCOME TO TRAVEL FOR 113 HOURS ON A HOT BUS WITHOUT ENOUGH FOOD TO ATTEND THE ACCRA GHANA TEMPLE FOR THE FIRST TIME.

Solomon's temple was built to
replicate the **temple in heaven.**

XII

PLAN OF SOLOMON'S TEMPLE.
with the two Inner Courts.
Eastern Entrance

Court of the Women

Court of the People

THE TEMPLE

Outer Court

PLAN OF HEROD'S TEMPLE.
NORTH

COURT

Court of the Gentiles

Court of Israel

PLAN OF
THE TABERNACLE

King Solomon spent

7 1/2 years

building a temple
that was so
impressive and
costly it still
ranks as one of the
most amazing
buildings ever
constructed
(1005 BC).

King Solomon built a baptismal font that rested on **twelve** metal oxen. It held enough water for 2,000 baths.

When Solomon dedicated his temple, he sacrificed 22,000 oxen and 120,000 sheep as an offering. That much meat could have fed 42 **million people** one meal each.

God sent a flame of fire from heaven to Solomon's temple to accept his sacrifice.

THE MODEST TEMPLE OF
ZERUBBABEL
REPLACED THE TEMPLE OF SOLOMON.

If you were born after 500 BC, you will never witness the splendor of Solomon's temple. Blame King Nebuchadnezzar for burning it to the ground.

Intertwined circles painted on the celestial room ceiling in the

Mount Timpanogos Utah Temple

were also used in Herod's temple.

HEROD'S TEMPLE GROUNDS WERE

4X

LARGER THAN THE ORIGINAL 10-ACRE TEMPLE SQUARE IN SALT LAKE CITY.

They represent eternity.

matches the dimensions of the wall built around the Temple of Herod.

King Herod *fixed up the* 500-year-old crumbling temple of **Zerubbabel** and *renamed it after* **himself**.

The wall around Temple Square closely

THE TEMPLE OF HEROD
IS THE TEMPLE
JESUS VISITED
DURING HIS LIFETIME.

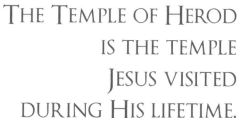

IT TOOK 5 TIMES LONGER TO BUILD THE SALT LAKE TEMPLE (40 YEARS) THAN THE COLOSSEUM IN ROME (8 YEARS).

LABORERS WORKED FOR **5 YEARS** TO COMPLETE THE HALF-MILE-LONG SANDSTONE AND ADOBE WALL SURROUNDING TEMPLE SQUARE.

In ancient America, the Prophet Nephi built a temple modeled after King Solomon's temple. While nephi was not as fancy, he used the finest materials and skills available.

After Jesus was resurrected, He came to America and visited the people at the temple.

Moses
OBEYED THE COMMANDMENT TO BUILD AN ELABORATE AND DETAILED PORTABLE TABERNACLE. **It was essentially a massive tent, but** only the finest materials were used.

Unless you live in Antarctica, there's

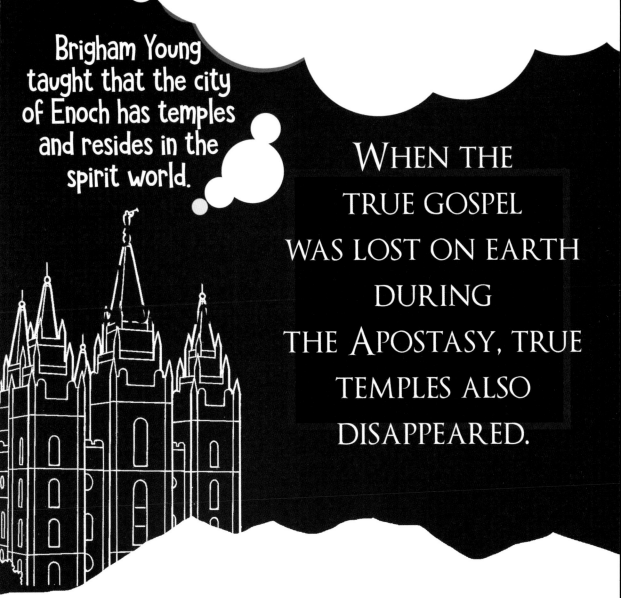

Brigham Young announced the Salt Lake Temple just 4 days after arriving in the valley.

There is one temple in Utah for every 117,000 Latter-day Saints.

20% of temples are exactly 10,700 square feet in size.

All 14 temples over 100,000 square feet are in North America.

1/3 of operating temples have names that start with the letters M, S, or C.

Starting in St. George, it would take only 19 hours to drive to all 17 temples in Utah.

THE
FIRST PRESIDENCY
APPROVES THE
FINAL DESIGN
OF EACH TEMPLE
DOWN TO THE
SMALLEST
DETAILS—SUCH AS
PAINT AND CARPET.

ALL LDS TEMPLES FOLLOW THE SPIRITUAL PATTERN GIVEN TO MOSES. DESIGNS CHANGE, BUT THE PATTERNS OF RITUALS ARE THE SAME.

THOUGH THE APIA SAMOA TEMPLE WAS DESTROYED BY A FIRE, THE HIGHLY FLAMMABLE FIBERGLASS ANGEL MORONI REMAINED UNHARMED, WAS SAVED, AND LATER WAS PLACED ATOP THE REBUILT TEMPLE.

FLAMMABLE

IN THE **FIRST** 150 YEARS
OF THE CHURCH OF JESUS
CHRIST OF LATTER-DAY SAINTS,
21 TEMPLES WERE BUILT.

138 TEMPLES WERE
COMPLETED IN THE
NEXT 38 YEARS.

Today, at least 85% of Latter-day Saints live within 200 miles of a temple.

Wow!
34
temples
were
dedicated in
the year
2000!

How did a temple end up in Communist China? Great Britain had leased (like renting) Hong Kong for 99 years, expiring in June 1997. The Hong Kong China Temple was finished just one year before China took control of Hong Kong again.

EVERY SUMMER, A LIFE-SIZED DOCTOR WHO TARDIS IS DISPLAYED ACROSS THE STREET FROM THE BOUNTIFUL UTAH TEMPLE, COMPLETE WITH A SIGN WELCOMING VISITORS TO TAKE A PHOTO.

In the Kirtland Temple meeting halls, there were pulpits on both ends and the seats were reversible.

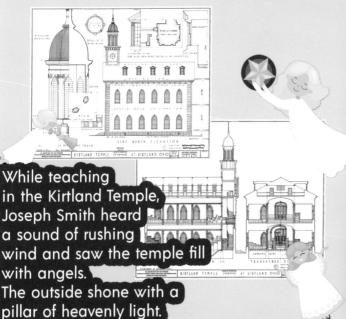

While teaching in the Kirtland Temple, Joseph Smith heard a sound of rushing wind and saw the temple fill with angels.
The outside shone with a pillar of heavenly light.

ANGELS WERE ALSO SEEN WALKING ON THE ROOF, DISAPPEARING AND REAPPEARING.

MUMMIES WERE ONCE ON DISPLAY TO VIEW, FOR A PRICE, IN THE KIRTLAND TEMPLE.

PRESIDENT JAMES E. FAUST SERVED A MISSION IN BRAZIL AND LATER BROKE GROUND FOR THE CAMPINAS BRAZIL TEMPLE, LOCATED ON JAMES EDRAS FAUST STREET.

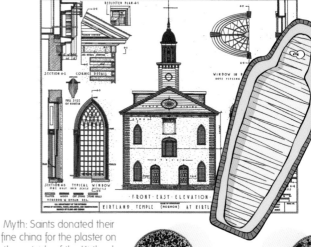

Myth: Saints donated their fine china for the plaster on the outside of the Kirtland Temple to make it sparkle.

Truth: Broken pottery and glass were used to create the shimmery plaster.

Way back in 1998 in **Kiev, Ukraine**, A TEMPLE WAS ANNOUNCED with only 5,000 **Latter-day Saints and one chapel in the entire country of 40 million** people. That's the same population as **California**.

25 FEET NARROWER THAN THE NEXT SKINNIEST TEMPLE, THE COPENHAGEN DENMARK TEMPLE IS ONLY 45 FEET WIDE.

To tour the

Kirtland Temple,

people paid a whopping

25 cents.

THERE WERE
24 PULPITS IN THE KIRTLAND
TEMPLE. EACH NAMED AFTER ONE
OF THE PLANNED 24 TEMPLES IN
THE FUTURE CITY OF ZION.

While olive oil is used for anointings today, in the Kirtland Temple, cinnamon oil was used.

In 1831, the Independence Temple in Missouri was the first temple site dedicated in this dispensation.

In 1837, 500 men spent around **2,000** hours excavating the foundation for a still yet-to-be-built temple in Far West, Missouri.

The cornerstones remain today, protected by glass.

NOW OWNED BY 3 DIFFERENT CHURCHES, THE 63-ACRE LOT INTENDED FOR THE INDEPENDENCE MISSOURI TEMPLE COST THE LDS CHURCH JUST $2 PER ACRE IN 1831.

In **1838**, Brigham Young dedicated a temple site in Adam-Ondi-Ahman, Missouri. Try to say Adam-Ondi-Ahman **5** times fast.

Early
Saints
"tithed"
time, money,
or valuables
to help
build the
Nauvoo
Temple.

THE NAUVOO TEMPLE WAS THE FIRST TO HAVE AN ANGEL FIGURE. IT WAS NOT CALLED MORONI AND WAS PLACED HORIZONTALLY ON A WEATHERVANE.

After completion, the temple was unsuccessfully listed for sale for $200,000 to fund the migration west. For a short time, the Catholic Church seriously considered the purchase.

Eventually, the Nauvoo Temple was sold for a few dollars to the Icarians.

30 PRESIDENTS OF THE UNITED STATES SERVED DURING THE 154 YEARS BETWEEN THE DESTRUCTION AND RECONSTRUCTION OF THIS TEMPLE.

The 30 capstones on the original Nauvoo Temple weighed about the same as 120,000 guinea pigs (1 pound each).

The original Nauvoo Temple charged $1.00 per ticket to attend the dedication.

A combination of a fire in 1848 and a tornado in 1850 destroyed the Nauvoo Temple.

Several miles of piping were installed to channel the concrete into the walls for the new Nauvoo Illinois Temple.

THE US MILITARY USES THE ANGEL MORONI AS THEIR OFFICIAL LDS SYMBOL.

Wilford Woodruff was visited by the Founding Fathers of the United States and pressed to complete their temple work. He got to work on it right away.

AN UNEXPECTED VISIT BY THE US ARMY CAN BE CREDITED WITH THE SALT LAKE TEMPLE RESTING ON A FIRM FOUNDATION TODAY.

IN FEAR, THE SAINTS HAD BURIED THE FOUNDATION — BUT LATER DISCOVERED IT WAS CRACKING AND REPLACED IT WITH **SOLID** GRANITE.

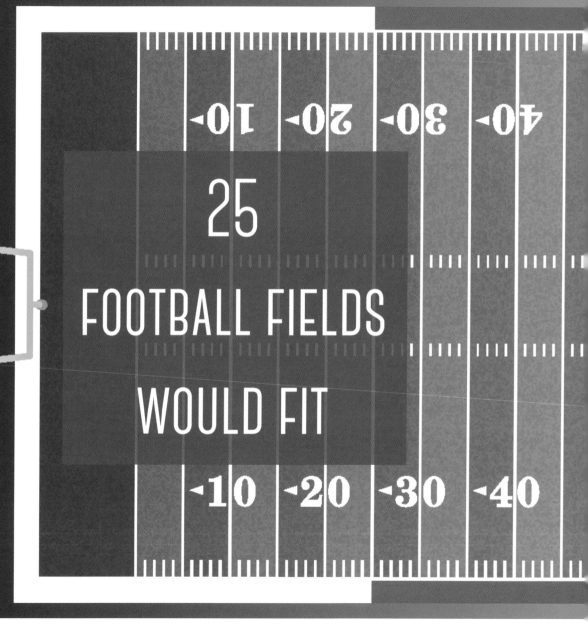

25
FOOTBALL FIELDS
WOULD FIT

ON TEMPLE SQUARE

If there were **18 kids** in one family, they could **all** be sealed to their spouses at the same time in separate sealing rooms in the **St. George Utah Temple.**

ALL 148 TEMPLE-TOPPER ANGEL MORONI STATUES HOLD TRUMPETS IN THEIR RIGHT HANDS.

The **heaviest** Angel Moroni statue weighs

4,000 pounds,

the same as 1,777 pizzas.

A temple maintenance worker's job description includes climbing scaffolding to clean bird droppings off the Angel Moroni statue.

THERE IS A TIME CAPSULE
IN THE BALL UNDER THE
ANGEL MORONI STATUE
ON THE SALT LAKE TEMPLE.

Myth: Temples have to face East. **Truth**: Temples often face East, but it isn't a rule.

THE WORLD'S FIRST MONUMENT HONORING BIRDS CAN BE FOUND ON TEMPLE SQUARE.

Business was **GOOD** for the shoe-covering bootie company when the Provo City Center Temple hosted 800,000 people during the open house.

Every temple has a time capsule placed inside of the cornerstone.

Sometimes a teenager is chosen to select the items to fill the box!

911

Emergency Call - calling...

mute

keypad

speaker

add call

hold

contacts

There are pipes in use under Temple Square made of tar and newspaper.

DURING THE DEDICATION OF THE ST. LOUIS
TEMPLE, SEVERAL PEOPLE CALLED 911 TO
REPORT THAT THE TEMPLE WAS ON FIRE.
FIREFIGHTERS ARRIVED TO FIND NO FIRE,
BUT MANY PEOPLE HAD SEEN THE
"SPIRITUAL FIRE" LIGHT UP THE TEMPLE.

You could hide a Boeing 747 (249 feet) and two stretch limousines (28 feet each) beside the Buenos Aires Argentina Temple, the longest temple at 311 feet.

The lights on the spire of the London England Temple help guide pilots into the nearby airport.

$843 NINETEENTH-CENTURY LOG CABINS (300 SQUARE FEET) WOULD FIT INSIDE THE SALT LAKE TEMPLE —THE WORLD'S LARGEST TEMPLE AT 253,000 SQUARE FEET.

FOR THE FIRST THREE YEARS OF OPERATION, THE SEATTLE WASHINGTON TEMPLE'S ANGEL MORONI HAD A FLASHING RED LIGHT AT ITS BASE TO WARN PLANES USING A NEARBY AIRFIELD.

Just before the Logan Utah Temple dedication in 1884, strangers hand-delivered a 3-day-old English newspaper full of temple-ready names and dates of over 60 deceased friends and relatives of Henry Ballard. With no internet or airplanes, that newspaper should have taken weeks to reach Utah.

EVERY ANGEL MORONI STATUE IS GILDED WITH GOLD, WHICH CONDUCTS ELECTRICITY PERFECTLY AND INVITES FREQUENT LIGHTNING STRIKES TO THESE BEACONS ON HIGH.

Lightning damage is usually minimal and not visible to the naked eye.

Since 2009, new Angel Moroni statues have two lightning rods—the second is in the trumpet.

ANGEL MORONI STATUES BUILT TODAY ARE PLACED ON COPPER POLES TO ACT AS LIGHTNING RODS, PROTECTING THE BUILDING, THE ELECTRICAL WIRING, AND THE PEOPLE INSIDE!

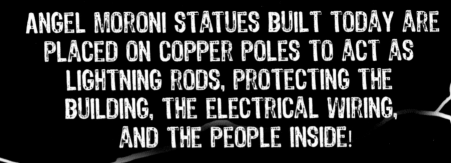

On May 22, 2016, the Angel Moroni on the Bountiful Utah Temple sustained significant damage from lightning. It was replaced 10 days later with a statue originally made for the nearly finished Meridian Idaho Temple.

A replica of the Angel Moroni on the Salt Lake Temple, owned by LDS Motion Picture Studios, can be found in the Church History Museum in downtown Salt Lake City.

Modern Angel Moroni statues weigh only 400 pounds—about as much as a football player or a full-grown reindeer.

THE TALLEST ANGEL MORONI STATUE, AT 18 FEET TALL, IS NEARLY

TWICE

THE HEIGHT OF THE BIBLICAL GIANT GOLIATH (9 FEET 9 INCHES) AND RESIDES ATOP THE WASHINGTON D.C. TEMPLE.

THREE MODERN TEMPLES HAVE ANGEL MORONI STATUES THAT ARE 6 FEET 10 INCHES, JUST 8 INCHES TALLER THAN LDS BASKETBALL STAR JIMMER FREDETTE.

Myth: Every LDS temple must have an Angel Moroni statue.

Truth:
Even though they are awesome, there is not an Angel Moroni requirement for temples.

On April 6, 1892, the Salt Lake Temple was capped with the world's first Angel Moroni statue.

The Salt Lake Temple's Angel Moroni is copper and THICKLY coated with gold.

ORIGINALLY, BLUEPRINTS CALLED FOR 2 HORIZONTAL ANGEL MORONI STATUES ON THE SALT LAKE TEMPLE.

THE SHORTEST ANGEL MORONI STATUES CAN BE FOUND ON 5 SMALL TEMPLES. MORONI APPEARS YOUTHFUL AND, AT 5 FEET 11 INCHES, IS THE SAME HEIGHT AS THE AVERAGE FINNISH MAN.

ANGEL MORONI STATUES NEED LOVING CARE AND ARE REPLACED OR REFURBISHED ABOUT EVERY 10-15 YEARS.

SUSPENDED 27 FEET UNDER THE SALT LAKE TEMPLE'S ANGEL MORONI IS A COUNTERBALANCE WEIGHT HEAVIER THAN

SIX 600-POUND ZEBRAS (4,000 POUNDS).

FOR 31 YEARS, THE PROVO UTAH TEMPLE DID NOT HAVE AN ANGEL MORONI STATUE.

THE VERNAL UTAH TEMPLE
MORONI STATUE WAS
ORIGINALLY PAINTED GOLD
BEFORE BEING COVERED
IN REAL GOLD LEAFING
4 MONTHS LATER.

THREE DIFFERENT TEMPLES' STATUES TEMPORARILY LOST THEIR TRUMPETS DUE TO EARTHQUAKES:

SANTIAGO CHILE, APIA SAMOA & TOKYO JAPAN.

BEFORE COMPLETION OF THE OAXACA MEXICO TEMPLE, A MASSIVE 7.6 MAGNITUDE EARTHQUAKE STRUCK, DESTROYING OVER 100 BUILDINGS. THE TEMPLE REMAINED IN PERFECT CONDITION.

DURING THE 2011 EARTHQUAKE IN TOKYO, JAPAN, THE ANGEL MORONI ROTATED

45 DEGREES.

HIS NEW VIEW WAS QUICKLY CORRECTED.

The famous sculptor Cyrus Dallin was not LDS and did not believe in angels,

but he chose to sculpt the Angel Moroni as a sign of the Restoration of the Gospel.

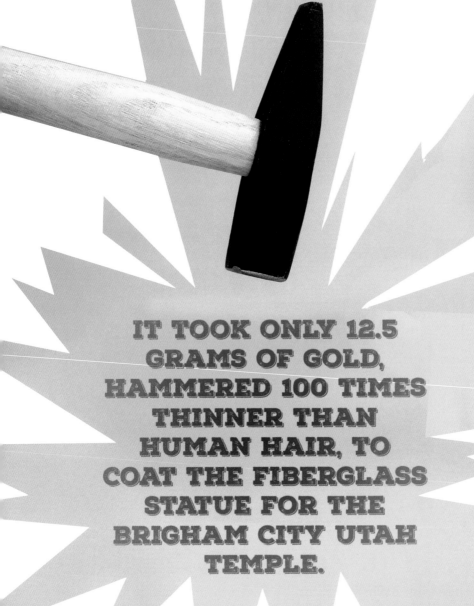

IT TOOK ONLY 12.5 GRAMS OF GOLD, HAMMERED 100 TIMES THINNER THAN HUMAN HAIR, TO COAT THE FIBERGLASS STATUE FOR THE BRIGHAM CITY UTAH TEMPLE.

Ten of the Angel Moroni statues hold something in their left hands, either a scroll or golden plates.

At the Los Angeles California Temple, the 15-foot Angel Moroni statue has Native American features and wears sandals, a headband, and Mayan-inspired clothing. All others wear flowing robes.

After sculptor Millard Malin invited Apostle Matthew Cowley to carve his initials in the wet clay of the Angel Moroni's robe for the Los Angeles California Temple, his "stamp of approval" was allowed to stay.

APPROVED
APPROVED
APPROVED

Upon being told that Moroni appeared to be drinking from his horn rather than blowing it, the sculptor of the statue for the Washington D.C. Temple, Avard Fairbanks, studied a model and fixed the lips to look more like a trumpet player. From the ground, his lips are not visible.

Most Angel Moroni statues face east, but at the Nauvoo Illinois Temple, both the temple and the statue face west toward the Mississippi River.

For one year after
the dedication in 1998,
a white Angel Moroni statue
adorned the top of the
Monticello Utah Temple.
It was later replaced with a
gold version for better
visibility on cloudy days.

Currently, only **11** temples
do not have an
Angel Moroni statue.

At the
Oakland California Temple,
visitors may climb
stairs to the top
of the *temple* and
walk around the
rooftop gardens.

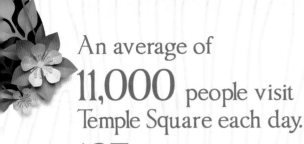

An average of **11,000** people visit Temple Square each day.

137 school buses would be needed to hold that many people.

Thanks to a faithful member following a dream, the majestic oak trees at the Houston Texas Temple were set aside and grown years in advance.

Entire families were called as missionaries to work in the pinery to harvest lumber for the first Nauvoo Temple.

300,000 plants and 200,000 bulbs are planted yearly in the Temple Square spring garden. Spend just one second looking at each plant, and you'll be there nearly 6 days to see them all.

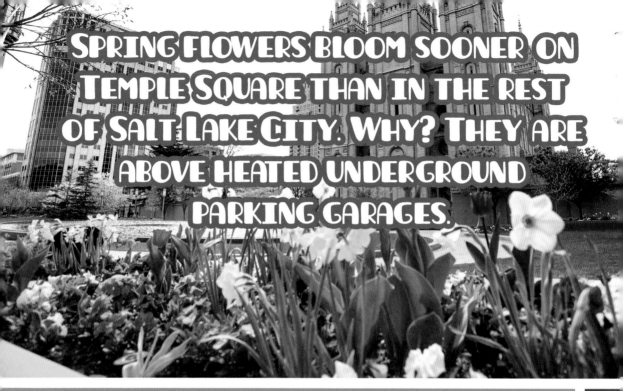

SPRING FLOWERS BLOOM SOONER ON TEMPLE SQUARE THAN IN THE REST OF SALT LAKE CITY. WHY? THEY ARE ABOVE HEATED UNDERGROUND PARKING GARAGES.

The Temple Square garden design changes EVERY year.

A TRUE GARDEN FOR THE WORLD, THE PLANTS ON TEMPLE SQUARE COME FROM 100 NATIONS.

The Salt Lake Temple once had a greenhouse attached to the side of the Garden Room.

THERE ARE TUNNELS UNDER TEMPLE SQUARE.

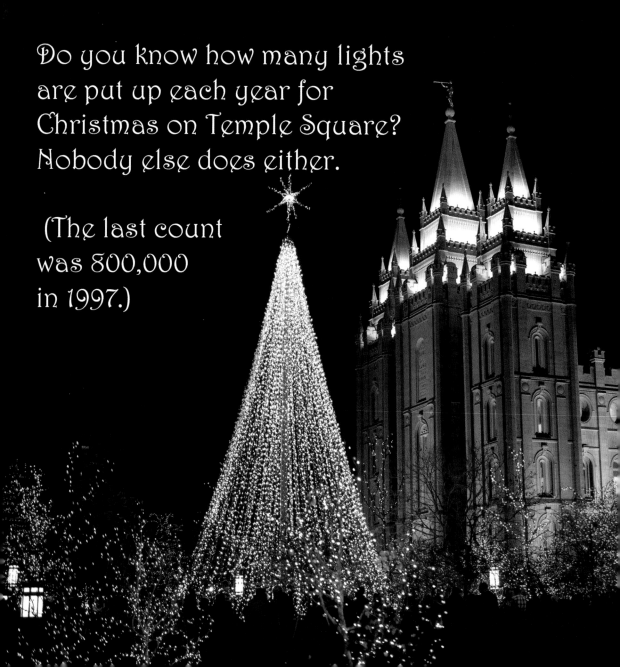

Do you know how many lights
are put up each year for
Christmas on Temple Square?
Nobody else does either.

(The last count
was 800,000
in 1997.)

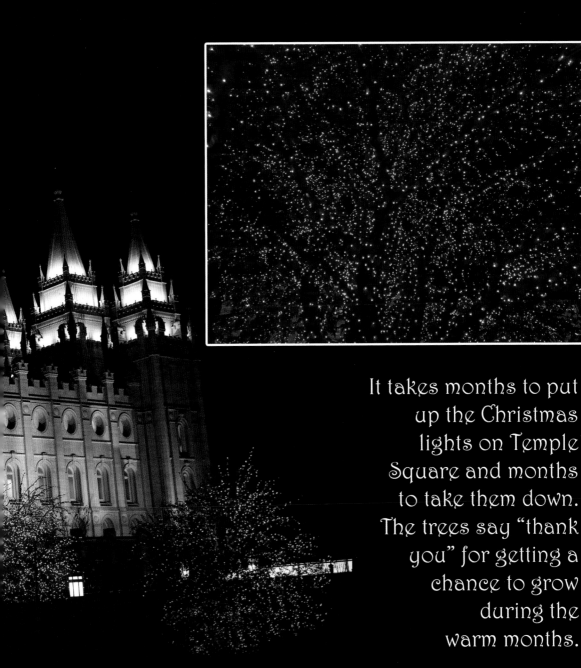

It takes months to put
up the Christmas
lights on Temple
Square and months
to take them down.
The trees say "thank
you" for getting a
chance to grow
during the
warm months.

The tallest temple,

the Washington D.C. Temple,

is 288 feet tall,

only 17 feet shorter

than the Statue of Liberty
(305 feet).

EARLY TEMPLES DIDN'T HAVE PARKING LOTS.

Many temples were first seen in visions, including those in Manti, Oakland, Switzerland, and New Zealand.

In the United States, there are fewer freestanding spiral staircases—with no central support—than fingers on your hands.

The Manti Utah Temple has 2 of these staircases.

THE MANTI UTAH TEMPLE
— COMPLETED IN 1888 —
COST ONE MILLION DOLLARS
IN MATERIALS ALONE.

DURING THE DEDICATION OF THE
MANTI UTAH TEMPLE,
DECEASED PROPHETS APPEARED
AND HALOS OF LIGHT LIT UP
THE SPEAKERS' HEADS.

THOSE IN ATTENDANCE HEARD AN
UNSEEN ANGELIC CHOIR FROM
BEHIND AND ABOVE THEM.

THERE ARE DINOSAURS IN THE MANTI UTAH TEMPLE—IN A MURAL.

Minerva Teichert stunned the world by painting a glorious 4,000 square-foot mural in just 30 days in the Manti Utah Temple, stopping twice a day for temple sessions to be held in that room! Most murals of this size take a year or longer.

WORKERS ON THE MANTI UTAH TEMPLE RECEIVED "NOT ONE DIME," AS DIRECTED BY BRIGHAM YOUNG.

There is a temple in **every** Spanish-speaking nation in South America.

THE TAIPEI TAIWAN TEMPLE HAS A BRILLIANT BLUE TILE ROOF.

Literally half a world apart, 12,379 miles separate the Asunción Paraguay Temple from the Taipei Taiwan Temple.

THE SHORTEST TEMPLE TRIPS HAPPEN AT THE KIEV UKRAINE TEMPLE—TRIPS FROM THE FRONT OF THE TEMPLE TO THE BACK ARE ONLY 84 FEET LONG.

FOR 8 YEARS, LATTER-DAY SAINTS IN NEW ZEALAND WORKED without pay TO BUILD THE HAMILTON NEW ZEALAND TEMPLE.

President Boyd K. Packer dedicated the Brigham City Utah Temple 82 years after attending elementary school on those very grounds.

MUSIC STANDS WERE USED TO SHOVEL SNOW DURING AN UNEXPECTED SNOWSTORM AT THE GROUNDBREAKING OF THE BILLINGS MONTANA TEMPLE.

Before a 2014 remodel, some people called the Ogden Utah Temple "The Ugly Temple." Others thought it looked like a UFO.

What do you think?

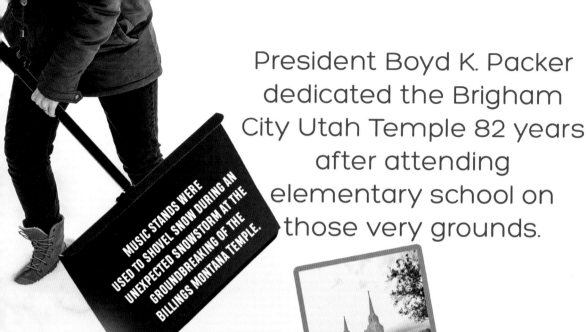

In 2017, someone accidentally crashed a drone on the top of the Draper Utah Temple.

The St. George Utah Temple is the only temple that had the groundbreaking the same day it was announced (November 9, 1871).

MORE TIME PASSED BETWEEN THE ANNOUNCEMENT AND GROUNDBREAKING FOR THE LOS ANGELES CALIFORNIA TEMPLE (14 YEARS, 6 MONTHS, AND 16 DAYS) THAN IT TAKES THE AVERAGE COLLEGE STUDENT TO COMPLETE A DOCTORATE DEGREE (12.5 YEARS).

The first Nauvoo Temple had a wooden baptismal font that could hold over 4,500 gallons of water when full. If you drank 8 glasses of water a day, that much water would quench your thirst for nearly 25 years.

Each ox is unique in the Brigham City Utah Temple baptistry.

The Kirtland Temple didn't have a baptismal font.

ANCIENT RECORDS REVEAL PROXY BAPTISMS FOR THE DEAD WERE PERFORMED AROUND AD 300 BY A CHRISTIAN GROUP CALLED MARCIONITES.

Myth: All temple baptismal fonts have 12 oxen.

Truth: Even though a font resting on 12 oxen is really cool and symbolic, there isn't an "oxen" rule, and some fonts do not have them.

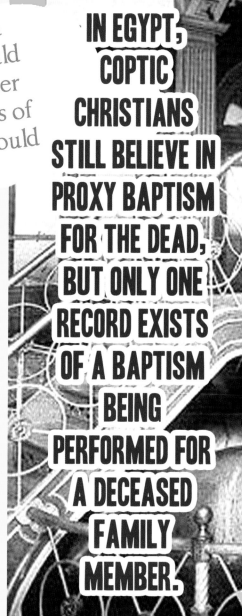

IN EGYPT, COPTIC CHRISTIANS STILL BELIEVE IN PROXY BAPTISM FOR THE DEAD, BUT ONLY ONE RECORD EXISTS OF A BAPTISM BEING PERFORMED FOR A DECEASED FAMILY MEMBER.

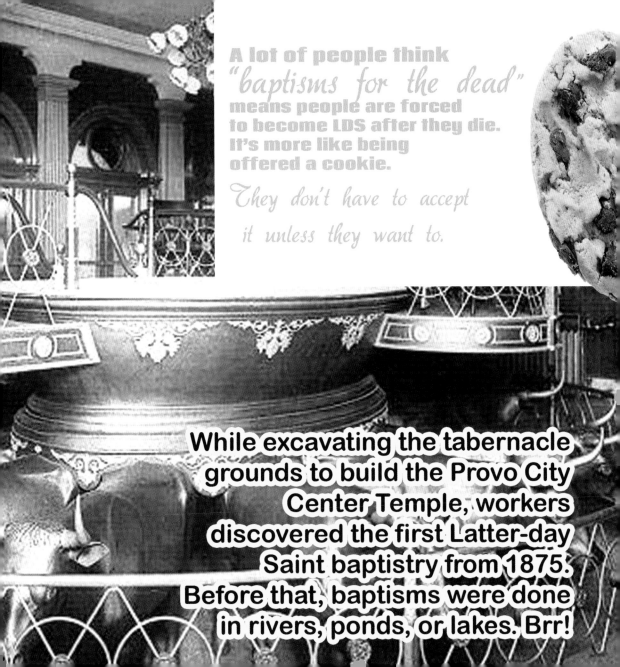

A lot of people think *"baptisms for the dead"* means people are forced to become LDS after they die. It's more like being offered a cookie.

They don't have to accept it unless they want to.

While excavating the tabernacle grounds to build the Provo City Center Temple, workers discovered the first Latter-day Saint baptistry from 1875. Before that, baptisms were done in rivers, ponds, or lakes. Brr!

THE VERNAL TABERNACLE WAS THE **FIRST** BUILDING LATER TRANSFORMED INTO A TEMPLE.

Smoking, drinking, and loud music are not allowed on temple construction sites.

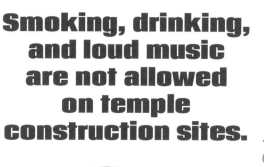

Each 5-piece sunstone for the first Nauvoo Temple cost the Saints $450, or $13,666 in today's money.

WHEN TEMPLES CLOSE TWICE A YEAR FOR CLEANING, THE MASSIVE CHANDELIERS ARE TAKEN DOWN AND THE CRYSTALS ARE SPREAD OUT AND CLEANED BY HAND.

Carpentry standards for temples are so high, only 1/64 of an inch variance is allowed.

That's about as thick as two hairs from your head!

When the Atlanta Georgia temple was remodeled, the crystal chandelier in the celestial room was crushed and turned into a gorgeous window.

The carpet in the Logan Utah Temple was handmade: sisters worked for 2 months to finish it.

MYTH: REVELATION LED TO MYSTERIOUS SHAFTS BEING BUILT IN THE SALT LAKE TEMPLE. LATER, THEY WERE THE PERFECT SIZE FOR ELEVATORS TO BE ADDED.

TRUTH: THE ARCHITECT LEARNED ABOUT ELEVATORS WHILE IN EUROPE AND PLANNED FOR THEM IN THE BLUEPRINTS.

It took 8 oxen 4 days to carry one stone to the Salt Lake Temple construction site.

The Assembly Hall was built using leftovers from the temple. Those were some nice leftovers.

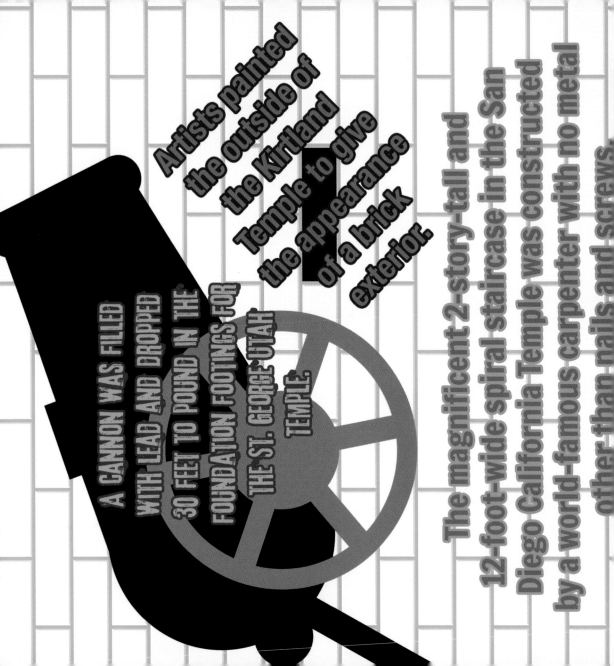

Artists painted the outside of the Kirtland Temple to give the appearance of a brick exterior.

A CANNON WAS FILLED WITH LEAD AND DROPPED 30 FEET TO POUND IN THE FOUNDATION FOOTINGS FOR THE ST. GEORGE UTAH TEMPLE.

The magnificent 2-story-tall and 12-foot-wide spiral staircase in the San Diego California Temple was constructed by a world-famous carpenter with no metal other than nails and screws.

Eleven temples are on streets with the word "temple" in their street name.

Real estate agents call the increase in home prices near temples the "Temple Effect."

In Idaho, it is illegal for ads to state that homes for sale are near a temple. One developer overcame this by using the name "Ensign" for the neighborhood by the Idaho Falls Temple.

KNOWN AS

America's Choir,

THE 360-MEMBER
MORMON
TABERNACLE CHOIR
AT TEMPLE SQUARE HAS
BEEN BROADCASTING
THEIR MUSIC SINCE 1929.

"THAT'S LONGER THAN ANY OTHER
PROGRAM IN THE HISTORY
OF THE WORLD."

Dave Jungheim spent 9 years and around $5,000 to build a 35,000-piece Lego Salt Lake Temple—topped with a gold-painted Obi-Wan Kenobi "Angel Moroni."

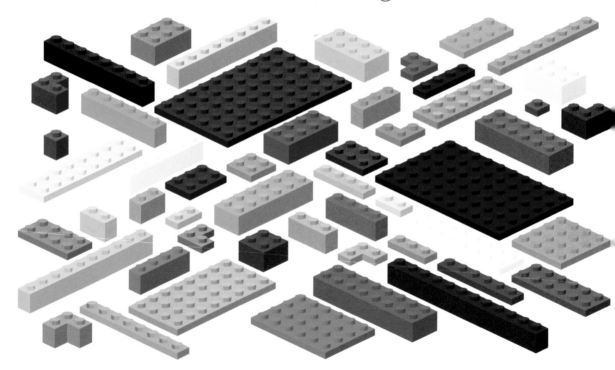

While it is true that James E. Talmage wrote *Jesus the Christ* in a room in the Salt Lake Temple, he did not actually LIVE at the temple.

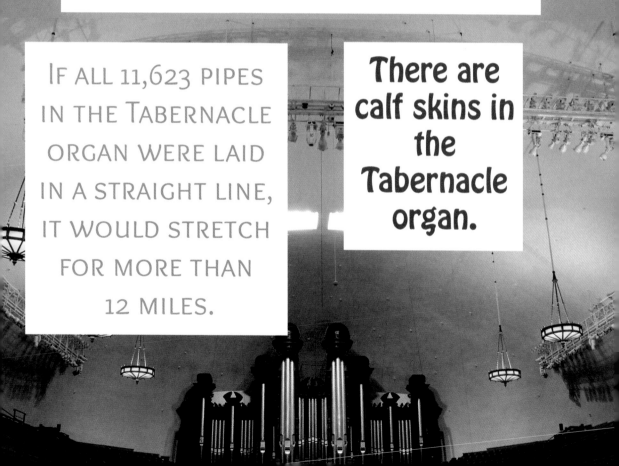

THE SALT LAKE TABERNACLE IS FAMOUS FOR 2 REASONS: (1) IT WAS BUILT WITHOUT ANY INTERNAL SUPPORTS, AND (2) A PIN DROPPED AT THE FRONT CAN BE HEARD PERFECTLY AT THE BACK.

IF ALL 11,623 PIPES IN THE TABERNACLE ORGAN WERE LAID IN A STRAIGHT LINE, IT WOULD STRETCH FOR MORE THAN 12 MILES.

There are calf skins in the Tabernacle organ.

The
design of
the Idaho
Falls
Temple
was
based on
the
architect's
vision in
which he
was shown
an
ancient
Nephite
temple.

If Cedar City had been named after the correct name for the abundant local trees, the temple there would likely be called the Juniper City Utah Temple.

JUNIPER BRANCHES, NOT CEDAR BRANCHES, ARE PAINTED IN THE CORNER OF THE TEMPLE'S CEILINGS.

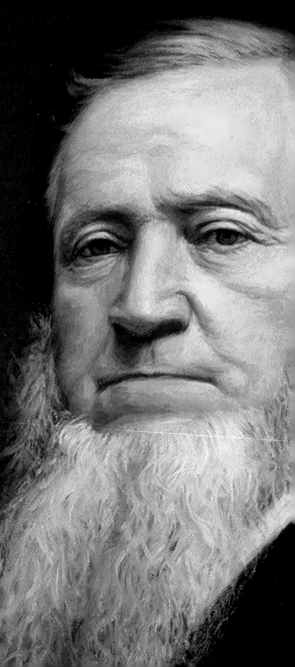

Brigham Young disliked the tower and dome on the St. George Utah Temple. 18 months after he died, a lightning strike damaged it severely. It was later replaced with a tall steeple.

Brigham Young declared wages "out of the question" for all who helped build the Logan Utah Temple, whether water boy or architect.

The Bountiful Utah Temple has an underground open-air garden atrium.

The busy city streets cannot be heard inside of the well-insulated Manhattan New York Temple, but because this multi-purpose building also houses a ward, basketball playing is not allowed during temple hours. It's too loud.

ANCIENT VIKING GRAVES WERE DISCOVERED ON THE SITE FOR THE STOCKHOLM SWEDEN TEMPLE.

THEY HAD TO BLOWTORCH THROUGH ICE FOR THE SWEDEN TEMPLE GROUNDBREAKING-TWICE!

Toes stay-toasty warm due to heated floors in the Anchorage Alaska Temple.

1% OF THE PEOPLE LIVING IN FINLAND ATTENDED THE OPEN HOUSE FOR THE HELSINKI FINLAND TEMPLE, MORE THAN DOUBLE OF WHAT WAS EXPECTED.

IF SANTA CLAUS WANTED TO FLY FROM THE NORTH POLE TO THE CLOSEST TEMPLE, HE WOULD TAKE HIS SLEIGH STRAIGHT TO ANCHORAGE, ALASKA (1,989 MILES).

Any South Pole residents wishing to visit the closest temple should head over to the Melbourne Australia Temple. It's only 3,603 miles away. Bring snacks.

North Pole

SANTA'S WORKSHOP

ELF VILLAGE

INDEER AIRFIELD

November 14, 1999: Halifax Nova Scotia and Regina Saskatchewan

April 23, 2000: Memphis Tennessee and Reno Nevada

May 21, 2000: Nashville Tennessee and Villahermosa Mexico

June 4, 2000: Montreal Quebec and San José Costa Rica

In just 7 short months, 4 temples shared the same dedication day with another temple.

The 18 smallest temples would fit inside of the Los Angeles California Temple (190,614 sq. ft.).

Donations from local members paid for the entire construction costs of the Jordan River Utah Temple.

Even the site for the Jordan River Temple was a gift to the Church—no tithing money was spent building it.

With a 750-person capacity, the Jordan River Utah Temple ordinance rooms can fit more people than any other temple—enough to fill a typical elementary school.

South Jordan, Utah, was the first city in the world with two LDS temples: Jordan River Utah Temple and Oquirrh Mountain Utah Temple. Provo, Utah, was the second: Provo Utah Temple and Provo City Center Temple.

Huge wedding party? The largest sealing room in any temple—at the Draper Utah Temple—holds 80 people.

The first couple married in the Kona Hawaii Temple was football legend Steve Young and his bride, Barbara Graham, on March 14, 2000.

Crushed coral and lava rock were mixed into the concrete for every part of the Laie Hawaii Temple—even the ceilings.

Famous singer and lifetime Latter-day Saint Donny Osmond was sealed to his wife in the Salt Lake Temple just 16 days after announcing his engagement (May 8, 1978).

500 weddings were scheduled for the Provo City Center Temple before it even opened!

The temple with the longest name is the

Kinshasa Democratic Republic OF THE CONGO TEMPLE (42 LETTERS).

That's a 16-syllable mouthful!

IN 2000, THE SUVA FIJI TEMPLE WAS MIRACULOUSLY DEDICATED WHILE REBELS HAD CAPTURED THE ISLAND'S LEADERS AND MARTIAL LAW HAD BEEN DECLARED.

IT never snows at the Guayaquil ECUADOR Temple, THE CLOSEST temple to the equator.

IN 2016, ENTIRE VILLAGES WERE DESTROYED IN THE STRONGEST TROPICAL STORM EVER RECORDED IN THE SOUTHERN HEMISPHERE, STRIKING JUST HOURS BEFORE THE SUVA FIJI TEMPLE REDEDICATION, EVERYONE WHO CAME WAS SAFE AND THE TEMPLE WAS UNHARMED.

EXPRESS DELIVERY

WITH A BUILD TIME OF JUST OVER 8 MONTHS, THE MONTICELLO UTAH TEMPLE HOLDS THE RECORD FOR THE FASTEST CONSTRUCTED TEMPLE.

During the 45 years between the announcement and dedication of the Salt Lake Temple, three other temples were completely built: St. George, Logan, and Manti.

Look closely at the murals in the Phoenix Arizona Temple and you'll find hidden pictures in the scenery, such as male and female cardinals and a gold miner.

Rainfall began shortly after President Hinckley prayed for it during a temple dedication in drought-stricken Mexico.

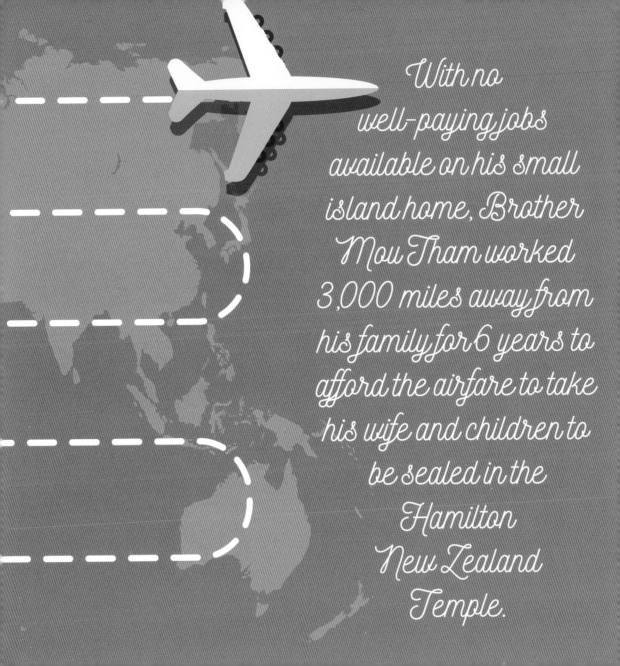

With no well-paying jobs available on his small island home, Brother Mou Tham worked 3,000 miles away from his family for 6 years to afford the airfare to take his wife and children to be sealed in the Hamilton New Zealand Temple.

The Salt Lake Temple has more rooms than the Taj Mahal –

170 versus 120.

Teni Keleotoni Temipale (Temple) was born in the Nuku'alofa Tonga Temple and delivered by a temple worker—a nurse who accidentally showed up 30 minutes early for a session. She delivered the baby and made the session too!

IN THE PATRON HOUSING OF THE JOHANNESBURG SOUTH AFRICA TEMPLE, A BABY WAS DELIVERED BY THE SAME SISTER, NOW A MISSIONARY, WHO HELPED THE NURSE DELIVER THE BABY IN TONGA.

JOSEPH TEMPLE BENNETT WAS BORN INSIDE OF THE SALT LAKE TEMPLE ON APRIL 7, 1893, AFTER HIS MOTHER SUDDENLY WENT INTO LABOR DURING THE TEMPLE DEDICATION.

Temple Momoh couldn't wait to be born and entered the world in the parking lot of the Aba Nigeria Temple. A week later, he was given a private tour.

In the **1960s**, the First Presidency seriously considered building a **traveling temple ship.**

Most of Houston was flooded in August 2017, including the Houston Texas Temple. For a few days, people could row boats to the front door.

Before the Manuas Brazil Temple was built, faithful members traveled for 4 days by boat on the Amazon and 3 days in buses on bumpy roads—a total of 2500 miles—to attend the temple.

ON NEW YEAR'S EVE, MISSIONARIES SERVING IN THE MANILA PHILIPPINES TEMPLE WATCH FIREWORKS FROM THE ROOFTOP OF THE TEMPLE!

MECHANICAL PROBLEMS WITH PRESIDENT HINCKLEY'S PLANE RESULTED IN TWO TEMPLES BEING DEDICATED ON THE SAME DAY FOR THE FIRST TIME: HALIFAX NOVA SCOTIA TEMPLE AND REGINA SASKATCHEWAN TEMPLE.

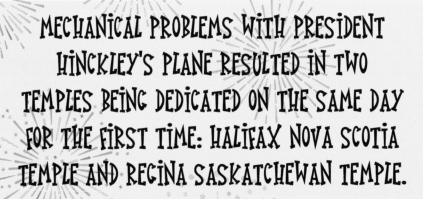

Fervent prayer by the First Presidency and the Quorum of the Twelve saved the Manila Philippines Temple from a group of rebel soldiers.

THE BERN SWITZERLAND TEMPLE WINS THE PRIZE FOR THE MOST FIRSTS: FIRST TEMPLE IN EUROPE, FIRST OVERSEAS, FIRST USING A TEMPLE FILM, AND FIRST WHERE ENGLISH WAS NOT THE MAIN LANGUAGE.

Some visitors to the

Paris France Temple

open house were visited by deceased family members while in the celestial room.

MYTH: LATTER-DAY SAINT WOMEN CUT AND DONATED THEIR HAIR FOR THE PLASTER ON THE KIRTLAND TEMPLE.

TRUTH: HORSE HAIR WAS USED, AS USUAL.

WHEN PRESIDENT GORDON B. HINCKLEY WAS BORN, THERE WERE ONLY 4 TEMPLES. HE GREW UP AND WENT ON TO DEDICATE 85 TEMPLES.

THE
Oquirrh Mountain Temple's

LAST-MINUTE NAME CHANGE FROM

THE

SOUTH JORDAN UTAH TEMPLE

REQUIRED NEW PROGRAMS FOR

THE DEDICATION.

At the Gilbert Arizona Temple, most people arrive in cars, but some ride their horses and tie them to a nearby rail before going inside.

25–30% of gravestones made in Salt Lake City include a temple on them.

The Winter Quarters Nebraska Temple was built right next to a Church-owned pioneer cemetery.

There are no temple names starting with the letters

X Y or Z.

The chandelier in the
Anchorage Alaska Temple
celestial room,
AT 700 POUNDS,
is heavier than 3 baby elephants.

Some members from Iquitos, Peru, sold their stoves and sewing machines to fund their six-day, 2000-mile trip to the Lima Peru Temple.

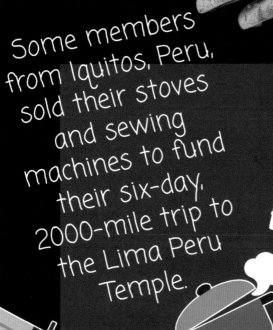

Construction workers at the Philadelphia Pennsylvania Temple were excited each Wednesday to receive 100 homemade cookies baked by local members.

The Salt Lake Temple is built from quartz monzonite, but it was nicknamed "temple granite" and the name stuck.

It would take a **CROW** only 2.5 minutes to fly from the **Provo Utah Temple** to the **Provo City Center Temple** (2.4 miles).

Only one temple in the world has a main entrance underground. You'll find it at the Provo City Center Temple.

THE CONSTRUCTION OF THE PROVO TEMPLE WAS PROPHESIED BY BRIGHAM YOUNG MORE THAN 100 YEARS BEFORE IT WAS DEDICATED.

The **HORROR** of watching the Provo Tabernacle burn was replaced with *joy* at the dedication of the **Provo City Center Temple**, built using the **Salvaged Tabernacle walls**.

IN 2005, HURRICANE KATRINA DEVASTATED LOUISIANA, BUT WHEN IT ENCOUNTERED THE BATON ROUGE LOUISIANA TEMPLE, THE STORM PARTED AND PASSED BY ON EITHER SIDE.

THE COPENHAGEN DENMARK TEMPLE WAS CONVERTED FROM A CHAPEL THAT ONCE SERVED AS A BOMB SHELTER.

MYTH: DURING THE ATTACK ON PEARL HARBOR, A JAPANESE PILOT TRIED THREE TIMES TO BOMB THE LAIE HAWAII TEMPLE BUT COULD NOT, AND LATER JOINED THE CHURCH.

TRUTH: THIS ACCOUNT CANNOT BE VERIFIED.

THE SAINTS IN SAO PAULO BRAZIL HAD NO MONEY TO DONATE FOR THE TEMPLE FUND, SO THEY GAVE THEIR GOLD AND SILVER AND PRECIOUS JEWELS OF ALL KINDS.

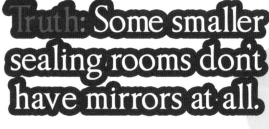

Myth: All sealing rooms must have mirrors on opposite sides to represent eternity.

Truth: Some smaller sealing rooms don't have mirrors at all.

Lima, Peru, is the first international city with two LDS temples.

At 40,000 square feet, the Rome Italy Temple is nearly 7 times larger than the nearby world-famous Sistine Chapel.

BEFORE JESUS CHRIST COMES AGAIN, THE NEW JERUSALEM TEMPLE WILL BE BUILT ON THE INDEPENDENCE TEMPLE LOT.

WHEN
HE
COMES AGAIN,
𝕵𝖊𝖘𝖚𝖘 𝕮𝖍𝖗𝖎𝖘𝖙
WILL REIGN FROM
HIS THRONE
IN THE
𝕹𝖊𝖜 𝕵𝖊𝖗𝖚𝖘𝖆𝖑𝖊𝖒
𝕿𝖊𝖒𝖕𝖑𝖊.

Special thanks to researchers Dellory Matthews and Bekalyn Craig, Angel Moroni expert Brian Olson, Tracy Daley for starting it all, Markie Riley for the fabulous graphics and design, the many friends and family who shared facts with me, and finally, my husband and children for allowing me to tell them hundreds of random temple facts and always believing in me.

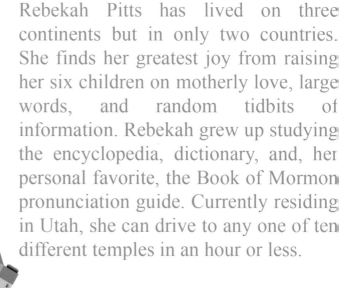

Rebekah Pitts has lived on three continents but in only two countries. She finds her greatest joy from raising her six children on motherly love, large words, and random tidbits of information. Rebekah grew up studying the encyclopedia, dictionary, and, her personal favorite, the Book of Mormon pronunciation guide. Currently residing in Utah, she can drive to any one of ten different temples in an hour or less.

Do you know which temple is home to an ancient Viking burial ground? Which temple had mummies on display? Which temple has more rooms than the Taj Mahal? Discover hundreds of fun and fascinating facts that will let you see LDS temples in a whole new light!

ALSO AVAILABLE AS AN
EBOOK

CFI

CEDAR FORT
Publishing & Media
AN IMPRINT OF CEDAR FORT, INC.

WWW.REBEKAHPITTS.COM